FANTASTIC
FIDGET SPINNERS

Originally published in the UK in 2017 as *Fidget Spinners* by
Macmillan Children's Books, an imprint of Pan Macmillan

ISBN 978-1-338-24937-8

12 11 10 9 8 7 6 5 4 3 2 1   17 18 19 20 21 22

Printed in the U.S.A.   40

First Scholastic printing, September 2017

Book design by Grant Kempster

FANTASTIC
FIDGET SPINNERS

Written by
EMILY STEAD

SCHOLASTIC INC.

CONTENTS

INTRODUCTION

FIDGET SPINNERS HAVE TAKEN THE WORLD BY STORM!

From playgrounds to offices, the whole world is in a spin about these propeller-shaped gadgets! So what is a fidget spinner, how does it work and where can I get my hands on one?

 THERE ARE DIFFERENT TYPES OF FIDGET SPINNERS, BUT THE MOST POPULAR IS A SMALL, THREE-ARMED GADGET.

 SPINNERS ARE EVERYWHERE! YOU CAN PICK ONE UP AT YOUR LOCAL TOY SHOP, SUPERMARKET OR ONLINE. FIDGET SPINNERS ARE IN DEMAND, SO YOU MAY NEED TO ORDER THE ONE YOU WANT.

HERE'S EVERYTHING YOU NEED TO KNOW ...

CAP

Whether you keep the caps on or pop them off, it's a question of choice. Many basic spinners are not fitted with caps. Some fidgeters say caps make for a smoother spin and keep out dust, while others prefer a simple spin with the caps removed.

ARM

The number of arms on a spinner can affect its speed. Two- or three-armed spinners usually offer faster spins, while spinners with more arms can be used for different tricks.

BEARINGS

Buy a spinner with the best quality bearings you can afford. Your spins will be smoother and your spinner will last longer.

CERAMIC BEARINGS are lighter, have less rolling resistance and will help get the maximum spin time out of the average spinner.

CERAMIC HYBRIDS are slightly cheaper, they are also light and can improve the spin times of the average fidget spinner.

STEEL BEARINGS are a good option if you need to replace your bearings on a budget.

HOW TO USE A FIDGET SPINNER

GETTING STARTED

1 Place your thumb and index or middle finger on the caps in the center of the spinner. (Try using your middle finger if you have smaller hands.)

2 Make the fidget spin by flicking it with the middle or index finger of the same hand, or with the hand that's free.

3 That's it! Now practice your spinning, flicking, balancing and playing—it's a great way to relax.

TIPS FOR SPINNER BEGINNERS

Try to buy a quality fidget spinner. This doesn't mean it has to be expensive, but be aware that some cheaper models can be noisy.

A pouch or carry case keeps dust and grease out of the bearings and your spinner in mint condition.

While metal spinners are pretty tough, dropping a plastic or wooden spinner on the ground could damage it.

Make sure you have plenty of space around you when you're practicing your tricks.

Steer clear of tricks that tell you to spin the spinner near your eyes or face.

BASIC TRICKS

THE FINGER SPIN

Once you've practiced the basic spin, try moving on to the Finger Spin.

1 Take the spinner in one hand. Place your thumb on the top cap and your index or middle finger on the bottom cap.

2 Keep the spinner in a horizontal position.

Use your free hand to give the spinner a good spin, then release your thumb.

 The spinner should spin freely on the pad of your finger.

 If you can manage this without wobbling, try the same trick using your thumb to balance the spinner.

THE TABLE TOP

This move is one of the first tricks to try with your fidget spinner. It's simple, but satisfying.

1 Place your spinner on a table top, or a hard, smooth surface.

2 Use one index finger to hold the spinner in place, then the other index finger to give it a spin.

3 Let go of the spinner and watch it whirl!

TIP: Try timing your spins and record your personal best! Then take on a friend in a timed challenge.

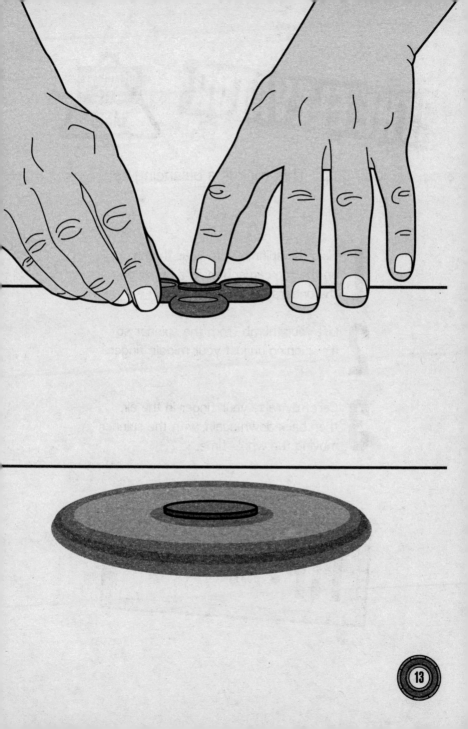

THE ELEVATOR

DIFFICULTY LEVEL

BASIC

Going up? This trick is a balancing act.

 1 Hold the spinner with your thumb on the top cap and middle finger on the underside cap, then flick.

 2 Lift your thumb from the spinner so it's spinning on just your middle finger.

3 Carefully raise your finger in the air, then back down again, with the spinner moving the whole time.

TIP: Try to keep this trick going for 60 seconds.

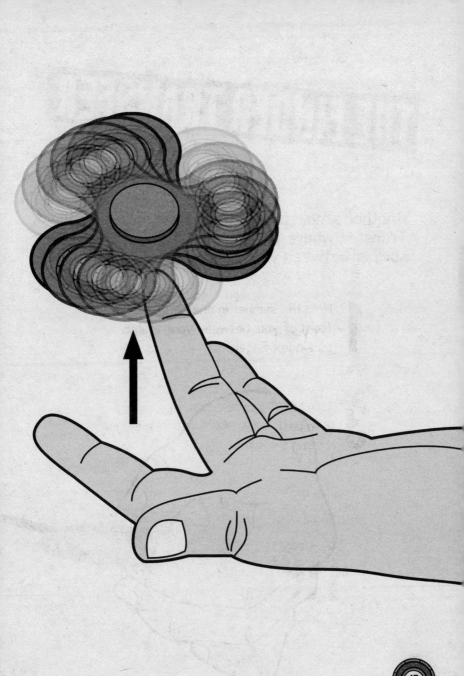

THE FINGER TRANSFER

Another simple trick is the Finger
Transfer, where you transfer the
spinner between your hands.

1 Hold the spinner in one hand out in
front of you, between your thumb
and index finger.

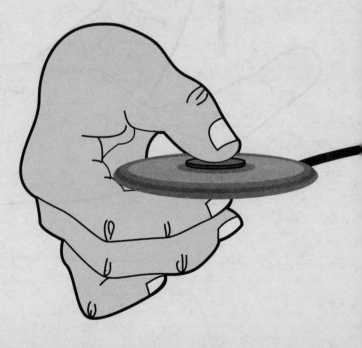

2 Flick the spinner so it gathers some speed.

3 While it's still turning, toss the spinner to your other hand. Use your index finger and thumb to catch it.

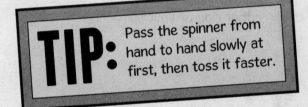

TIP: Pass the spinner from hand to hand slowly at first, then toss it faster.

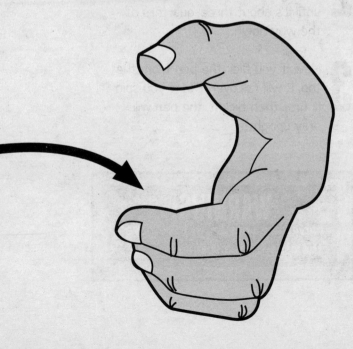

THE PEN PUSHER

For a super-fast spin!

1 Carefully pop off the caps from either side of your spinner.

2 Take a pen or a pencil and slide it through the spinner's central hole, until it's about three-quarters of the way down.

3 Now if you flick the pen from the top, it will fall over. But if you spin it first then flick it, the pen will stay upright!

WARNING!
Never use your teeth to remove the caps from a spinner.

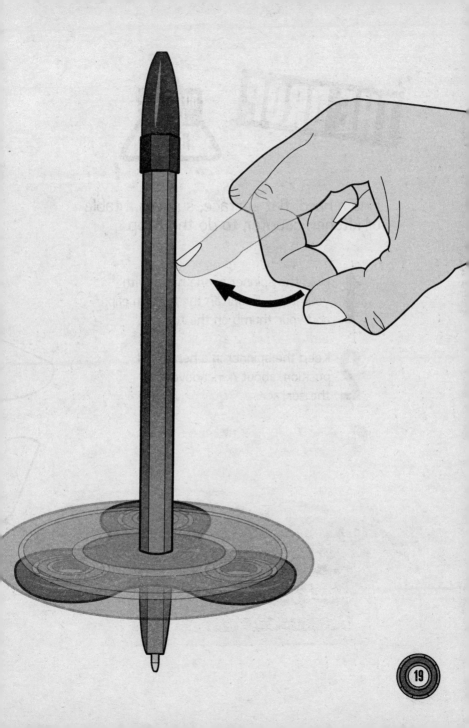

THE DROP

DIFFICULTY LEVEL

BASIC

Find a hard, flat surface, such as a table or kitchen counter, to do the Drop.

1 Hold the spinner in one hand, with your index finger on the bottom cap and your thumb on the top cap.

2 Keep the spinner in a horizontal position, about 4 in. above the surface.

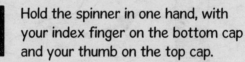

3 Use your free hand to get your spinner moving, then toss the spinner in front of you, onto the table. Releasing both fingers at the same time helps to keep the spinner steady.

4 The spinner should land smoothly on the table and continue its spin.

TIP: Super easy? Try a Double Drop using two spinners!

THE BOTTLE SPIN

DIFFICULTY LEVEL

BASIC

You'll need an unopened bottle of water or soft drink to perform the spin.

1 Place your spinner on the lid of the bottle, and hold it in place with your index finger.

2 Use your free hand (index or middle finger) to spin the spinner.

3 Release the finger holding the spinner, then watch your spinner spin hands-free!

4 Try timing your spins using a stopwatch, or challenge a friend to a bottle spin-off!

TIP: Choose a bottle that has a flat bottle top.

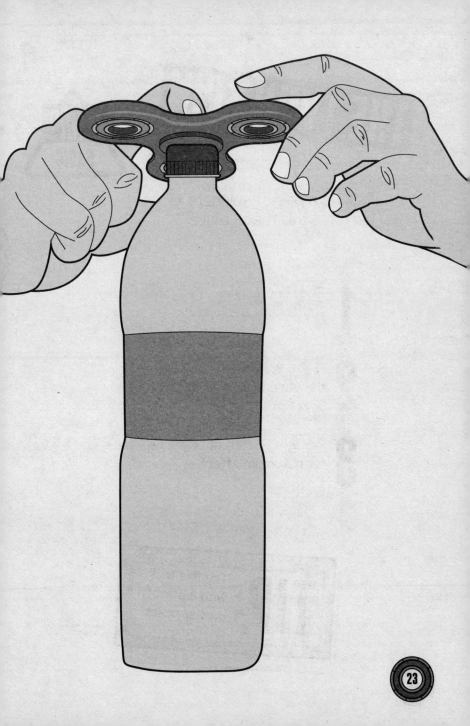

THE TWIN SPIN

DIFFICULTY LEVEL
BASIC

Pick up a pair of spinners to perform this mega move!

1 Place one spinner on top of the other, so the caps are touching.

2 Flick one spinner one way, then spin the other spinner in the opposite direction.

3 Try using different colored spinners for maximum effect.

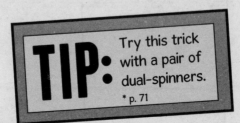
TIP: Try this trick with a pair of dual-spinners.
* p. 71

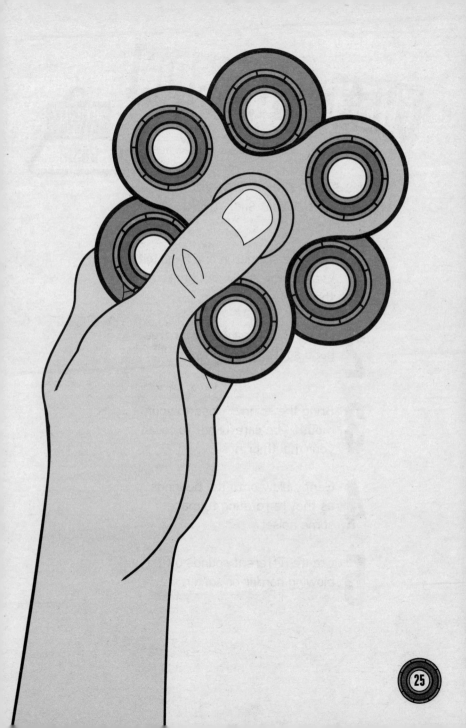

THE 'COPTER SPIN

DIFFICULTY
LEVEL
BASIC

Make some noise with your
spinner with this slick trick!

1 Hold the spinner in one hand with
your thumb and index finger on
the caps.

2 Flick the spinner with your free
hand so it's spinning fast.

3 Bring the spinner close to your
mouth—be careful not to touch
your mouth or nose.

4 Gently blow onto the bearings
as they're rotating to make
some noise!

5 Create different sounds by
blowing harder or softer.

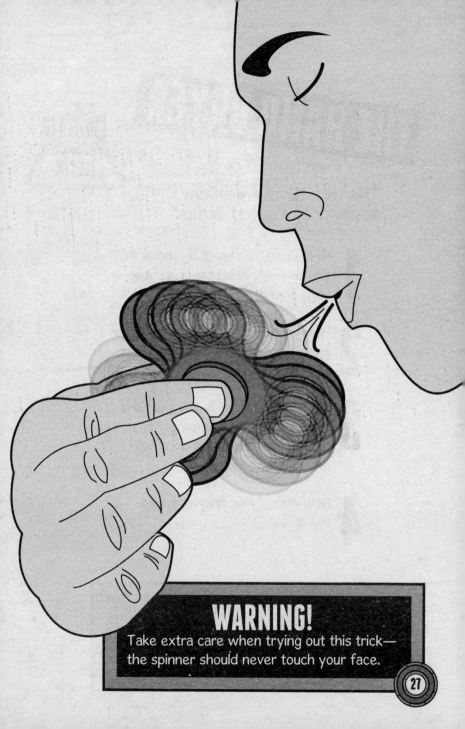

WARNING!
Take extra care when trying out this trick—
the spinner should never touch your face.

THE HAND DRYER

DIFFICULTY LEVEL
BASIC

This trick turns almost any spinner into a speed demon!

1 Find an electric hand dryer, the type you see in your school or a public bathroom (it needs to be pretty powerful).

2 Hold your spinner with the thumb and index finger of one hand, as shown.

3 Place your spinner below the hand dryer's jet of air. Remember to push the start button if the dryer isn't automatic!

4 Now watch your spinner speed like crazy!

WARNING!
Avoid any damage to your spinner—don't let it touch the hand dryer.

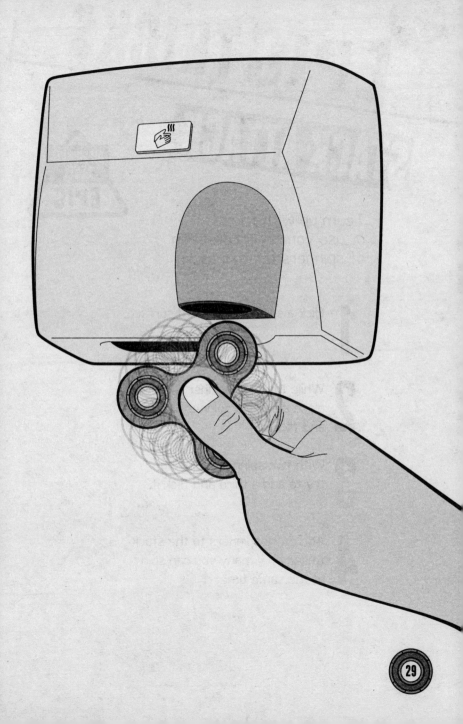

EPIC TRICKS

STACK ATTACK

DIFFICULTY LEVEL
EPIC

Team up with friends
or use your own collection
of spinners for this trick.

1 Flick a spinner on a hard surface.

2 While the first spinner is moving,
place a second spinner on top
and flick.

3 With two spinners spinning,
try to add a third and flick it.

4 Add more spinners to the stack
to see how many you can spin
at the same time.

THE STICK TRICK

DIFFICULTY LEVEL
EPIC

If you found the Elevator too easy, the Stick Trick will take your skills to the next level.

1 Find a long stick or rod with a flat tip.

2 Hold the spinner in one hand and flick it hard to create some speed.

3 Using your free hand, pick up the stick and carefully transfer the spinner to the flat tip. It should be spinning the whole time.

4 Slowly raise the stick up and down. Be careful not to hit the ceiling.

THE STRING SPINNER

DIFFICULTY
LEVEL
EPIC

It's a string thing.

 1 Carefully pop off the caps from either side of your spinner if your spinner has caps.

 2 Take a pen or a pencil and slide it through the spinner's central hole, until it's about three-quarters of the way down.

 3 Tightly wind a piece of string (about 2 ft long) to the shorter end of the pen, as shown.

 4 Set your spinner spinning with one hand, while holding the end of the string with the other hand.

5 Tug the string hard and look out for a double spin. Spectacular!

WARNING!
Never use your teeth to remove the caps from a spinner.

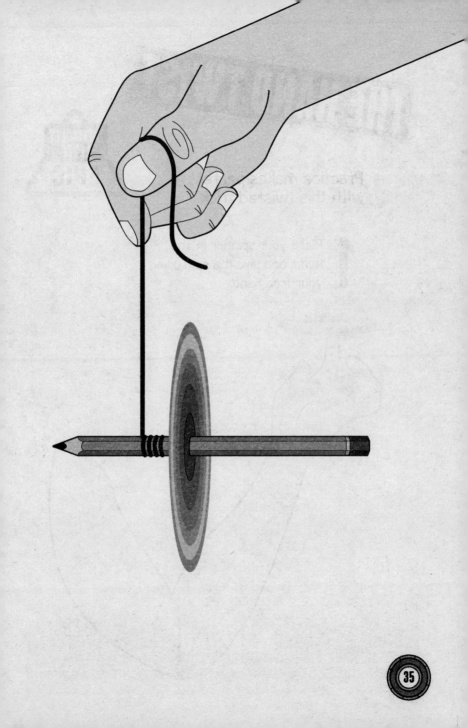

THE HAND TWIST

DIFFICULTY LEVEL
EPIC

Practice makes perfect
with this twisted trick.

1 Place your spinner in one
hand, and give it a spin using
your free hand.

2 Rotate your wrist, bring your elbow up above your spinner, then pull your hand around in a quick movement so the spinner is back in the position in which you started.

3 Try to keep your spinner in a horizontal position at all times.

TIP:

This trick is probably the toughest challenge so far. Keep practicing!

THE REVERSE FLIP

DIFFICULTY
LEVEL
EPIC

Could it be magic?

1 Hold the spinner by one of its arms, using your thumb and middle finger.

2 Position the spinner towards your body, with your thumb pointing downwards.

3 Flick the spinner up from the arm and catch it in the center caps, using a pinch grip.

4 This trick should be a quick, almost-magical flick that starts off with one grip and ends up in another.

TIP: Try the Reverse Flip with your eyes closed. Trust your hands to make the catch.

THE VERTICAL TOSS

Show this toss who's boss!

DIFFICULTY LEVEL EPIC

1 Hold your spinner in one hand, with your thumb and index finger on the caps.

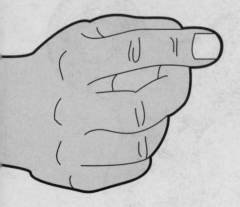

WARNING!
Make sure you have plenty of space before trying out this trick.

2 Now turn the spinner so it faces your body in a vertical position, with your thumb closest to you.

3 Spin the spinner using your free hand, then toss the spinner from hand to hand, keeping it spinning in a vertical position.

4 Catch the spinner by the cap using a pinch grip. If you aim to catch it just below the cap, the spinner should fall into your fingers perfectly.

THE KICK

DIFFICULTY LEVEL
EPIC

Keep your shoes on for
this move.

1 Make sure you have plenty
of room for this trick.

2 Toss the spinner up a little,
then let it fall.

3 Cushion the spinner's landing
using the inside of your foot,
then try to catch the spinner.

4 Avoid using your ankle to tap
the spinner.

5 If you're right-footed, use your
right foot and left foot if you're
left-footed. Or try mixing it up
to take this trick to the next level.

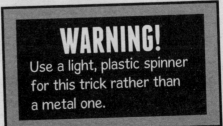

WARNING!

Use a light, plastic spinner
for this trick rather than
a metal one.

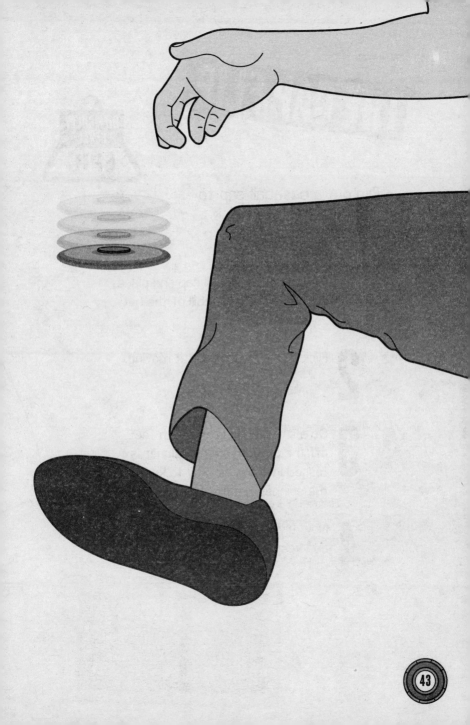

THE CAP FLIP

DIFFICULTY
LEVEL
EPIC

Dig out a baseball cap to
perform this epic trick.

1 Put on your baseball cap and place
your spinner on the bill of the hat.

2 Flick the spinner to get it moving.

3 Do a small jump, lifting both feet
off the ground, so the spinner is
tossed into the air. Try to keep
the spinner in a horizontal position.

4 Now try to catch the spinner
and keep it rotating.

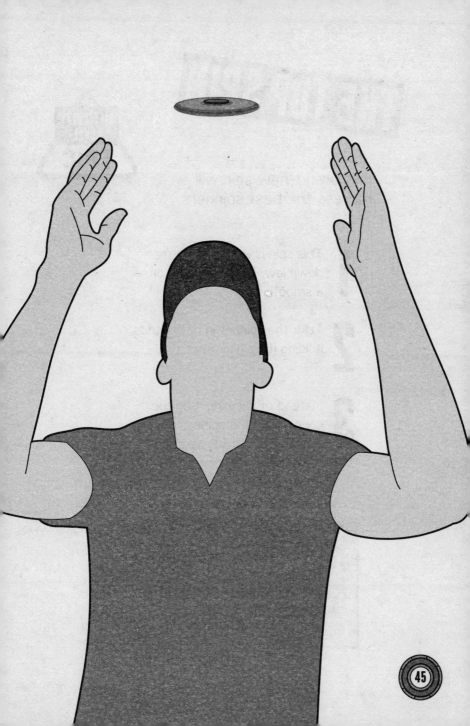

THE TOP SPIN

DIFFICULTY
LEVEL
EPIC

This brand-new spin will
impress the best spinners.

1 This spin is easiest if you're
down low, so try spinning on
a smooth floor.

2 Take the spinner in both hands,
holding it by two arms.

3 Instead of spinning it by the
caps, stand the spinner on one
arm and flick it to make it
rotate like a spinning top.
A simple but sweet spin!

WARNING!
This trick works best with
a plastic spinner. Only use
a metal spinner outside.

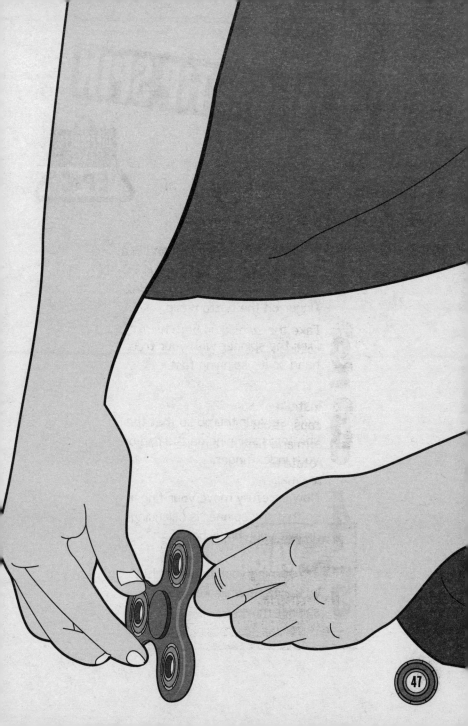

THE FINGERTIP SPIN

DIFFICULTY LEVEL
EPIC

Not as easy as it sounds . . .

1 Hold the spinner in one hand in a horizontal position, with your thumb on the top cap and index finger on the bottom cap.

2 Flick the spinner with your free hand so it's spinning fast.

3 Release your thumb so that the spinner is spinning on the pad of your index finger.

4 Now carefully move your finger, so that the spinner is balancing on just your fingertip.

5 Try turning your finger slightly left or right while keeping the spinner moving.

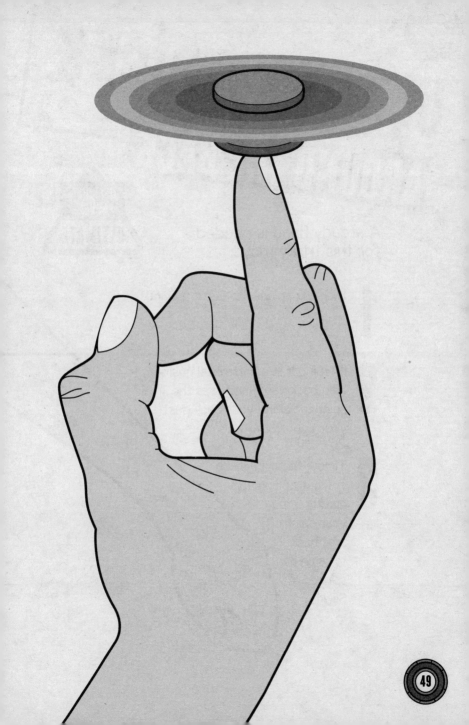

ULTIMATE TRICKS

AROUND THE BACK

DIFFICULTY LEVEL ULTIMATE

A steady hand is needed for this tricky move.

1 Flick the spinner to get it moving.

2 Keeping it in a horizontal position, lean backwards and toss the spinner behind your back past your opposite arm.

3 Throw the spinner up in front of you and quickly bring your spinning arm back to catch the spinner. Slick!

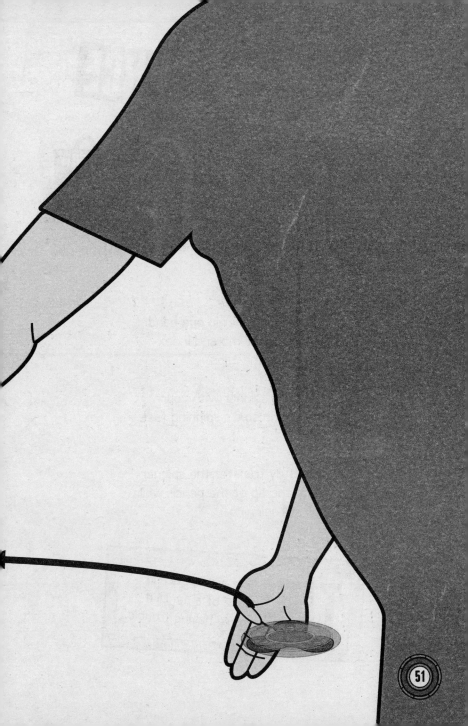

THE PENCIL BALANCE

This trick will really test
your spinner skills.

DIFFICULTY
LEVEL
ULTIMATE

1 Pick out a pencil with a fairly
blunt end.

2 Hold the spinner in one hand
with your thumb and index
finger on the caps.

3 Flick the spinner with your
free hand so it's spinning fast.

4 Carefully transfer the spinner
onto the tip of the pencil, while
it's still spinning.

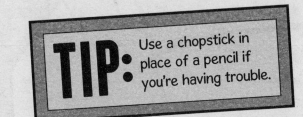

TIP: Use a chopstick in
place of a pencil if
you're having trouble.

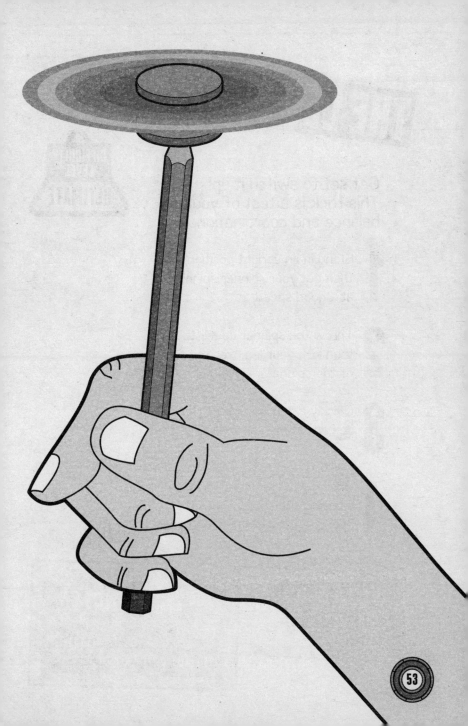

THE LEG SWITCH

DIFFICULTY LEVEL

ULTIMATE

Get set to switch it up!
This trick is a test of your
balance and coordination.

 Stand in an upright position,
then get your spinner spinning
at a good speed.

 Throw the spinner up a little,
then kick your leg over the top
of the spinner.

Quickly catch the spinner by
its caps in the same hand.

 Once you've mastered this, try
catching the spinner with the
opposite hand, then kicking your
other leg over the top.

WARNING!

Make sure you have plenty
of space, away from any
furniture, for this trick.

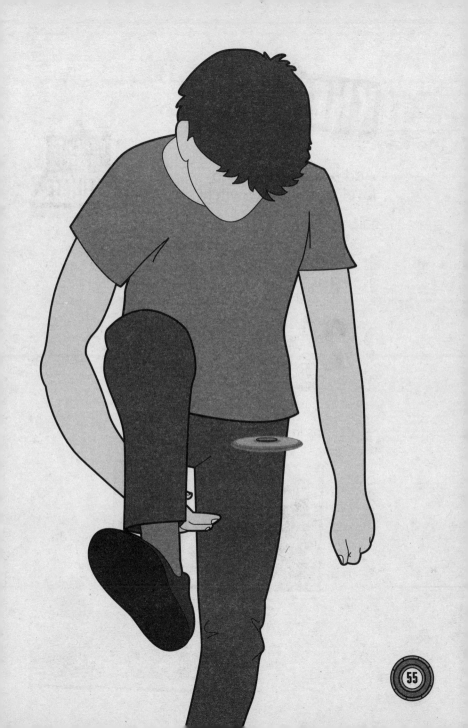

KNEES UP

Add a knee bounce to
level up the Leg Switch!

DIFFICULTY
LEVEL
ULTIMATE

1 Try the Leg Switch trick again,
spinning the spinner under
one leg.

2 This time, instead of catching
it with your hand, allow the
spinner to bounce off your
knee before catching it. Epic!

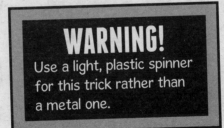

WARNING!
Use a light, plastic spinner
for this trick rather than
a metal one.

THE HIGH TOSS

Make some room before
you try out this trick.

DIFFICULTY
LEVEL
ULTIMATE

1 Hold the spinner in one hand,
with your thumb on the top
cap and index finger on the
bottom cap.

2 Get the spinner moving with
a hard spin.

3 Toss the spinner in the air in
front of you, so it travels
above head height.

4 Catch the spinner in a pinch
grip with your opposite hand,
with the spinner still rotating.

WARNING!

Take care when throwing your spinner above head
height, and make sure you have plenty of space.

THE KNUCKLE DOWN

Knuckle down and practice this handy trick.

DIFFICULTY LEVEL
ULTIMATE

 Hold the spinner in one hand, with your thumb on the top cap and index finger on the bottom cap.

 Spin the spinner hard using your free hand, then release your thumb.

 Toss the spinner up, then quickly flip over your hand, so that your knuckles are facing upwards.

 Bend your index finger up slightly, then try to catch the spinner on the knuckle of the same finger.

 This move needs to be fast and precise—it might take a few tries to get right.

Once you can do this easily, try the trick in reverse by tossing the spinner from your knuckle to land back on the pad of your index finger.

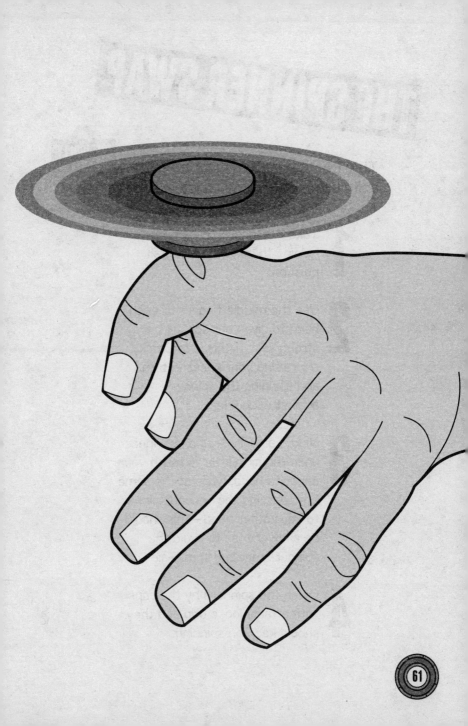

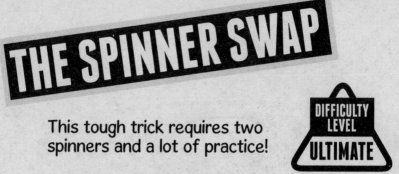

THE SPINNER SWAP

This tough trick requires two spinners and a lot of practice!

DIFFICULTY LEVEL
ULTIMATE

1 Take a spinner in each hand, holding them in a horizontal position.

2 Use the middle fingers of each hand to give your spinners a strong spin. If this is too tricky, try raising your knees in turn and spinning the spinner against each knee.

3 Next, carefully toss one spinner up in the air a little to reach your opposite hand, while at the same time passing the second spinner to your other hand—this should be a lower toss to avoid the spinners meeting in mid-air.

4 Catch the spinners by the caps with a fairly loose grip and they should keep on spinning.

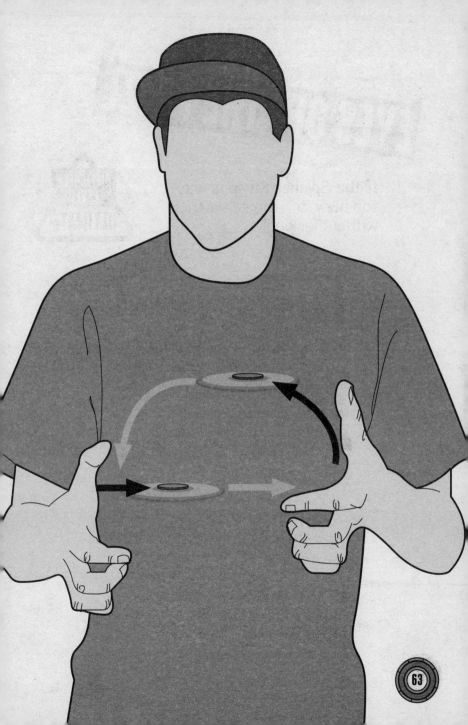

EYES OFF THE PRIZE

If the Spinner Swap is way too easy, try the same trick without looking!

DIFFICULTY LEVEL
ULTIMATE

1 First, practice tossing one spinner from hand to hand without looking—trust your hands to make the catch!

2 Next try the Spinner Swap trick again, but this time look straight ahead or wear a blindfold. This trick is tougher than it sounds.

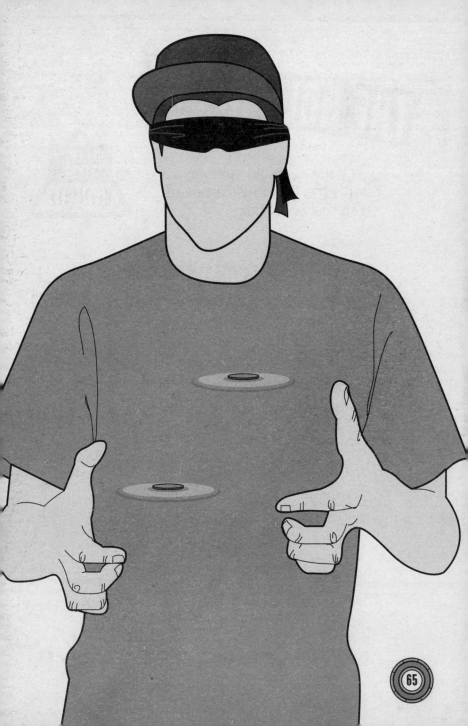

THE HOLE IN ONE

Try using an old spinner
with the bearings removed
for this cool trick.

DIFFICULTY
LEVEL
ULTIMATE

1 Hold the spinner in one hand,
with your thumb on the top cap
and middle finger on the bottom cap.

2 Spin the spinner hard using
your free hand.

3 While the spinner is still rotating, try to stop it dead by inserting the index finger of your free hand into one of the holes in the arms, where the bearings would normally be.

THE CLAP AND TRAP

This trick is a true test of your reaction times.

DIFFICULTY LEVEL
ULTIMATE

1 Hold the spinner in one hand, with your thumb on the top cap and index finger on the bottom cap.

2 Spin the spinner hard using your free hand.

3 Toss the spinner in the air, then clap your hands together behind your back and bring one hand back in front to make the catch.

4 This should be a quick movement.

5 Once you've mastered this, try adding a clap in front of you after the backwards clap before catching the spinner.

TOP 10 FIDGET SPINNERS

There are so many cool spinner designs out there that it's hard to choose a favorite. Check out ten of the best, then decide which spinner you'd like to take for a test spin.

TRI-SPINNER

The original and best?

These pocket-sized propellers are compact and usually lightweight. They are great for tricks and spin smoothly too. The perfect starter spinner.

DUAL-SPINNER

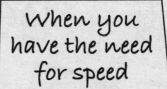

When you
have the need
for speed

While tri-spinners come
out on top for tricks, dual
spinners are super-fast.
These two-armed spinners
can turn for up to six
minutes. Beat that!

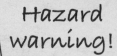

Hazard warning!

RADIOACTIVE SPINNER

This spinner looks like a radiation-hazard symbol, but it's definitely not nuclear! This sleek design of this spinner keeps it moving for five minutes. Smooth!

NINJA SPINNER

This twist on a tri-spinner looks cool and spins well. Stay away from spinners with sharp edges—spinner injuries are not a good look.

Spin like a ninja!

GLOW-IN-THE-DARK SPINNER

Go with the glow!

Show off your tricks after lights out with this luminous spinner. It has all the features of a normal tri-spinner, with added glow-in-the-dark awesomeness!

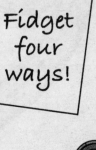

QUAD-SPINNER

Fidget four ways!

With an extra arm, the quad spinner offers even more ways to fidget. For smaller hands, it can be a little clunky. Other spinners work better for hard-surface spins.

SPINNING WHEEL

The wheel deal!

The spinning wheel keeps on rollin' for an average spin time of four minutes. With a metal rim, it's heavier than other designs, making it less portable, but it's a solid spinner all the same.

FLOWER POWER

Take five!

Flower or starfish, whatever this five-armed
spinner reminds you of, it's a winner of a
spinner. Its spin time is OK, at around two and
a half minutes, so try using it for tricks.

WOODEN FIDGET

Wooden spinners are a fun option for fidgeters who like to stand out in a crowd. Be sure to take care of your spinner, as some lightweight wooden versions are not as tough as plastic spinners.

Wood you believe it!

BATMAN SPINNER

The superhero's spinner

This batarang spinner not only looks cool, it has a good spin time and is as smooth as the Caped Crusader himself. Boom!

SPINNER HACKS

Want your spinner to look cooler? Spin faster? Or how about making a DIY spinner from scratch?

Try these upgrades to create a one-of-a-kind spinner that will be the envy of your friends!

FLYING COLORS

WARNING!

Adult supervision is recommended when sharp-pointed items, such as craft knives or scissors, are in use.

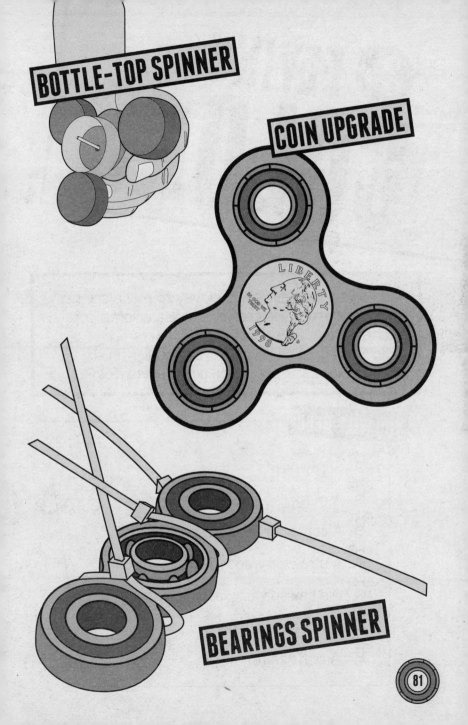

BOTTLE-TOP SPINNER

COIN UPGRADE

BEARINGS SPINNER

81

FLYING COLORS

Adding some color is a cool way to make spinner stand out from the crowd. Choose colored spray paints—your favorite shades, sports team colors, or gold or silver for a metallic finish. Neon paints are great for night spins, too.

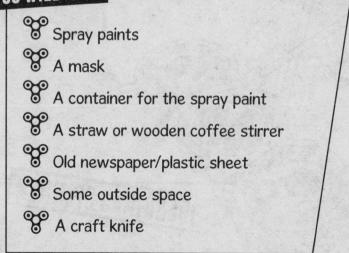

YOU WILL NEED:

- Spray paints
- A mask
- A container for the spray paint
- A straw or wooden coffee stirrer
- Old newspaper/plastic sheet
- Some outside space
- A craft knife

How to Make:

1 Create a painting area by laying down old newspapers or a plastic sheet.

2 Ask an adult to spray some spray paint into an old container. This is a messy job that should be done outside or in a room with plenty of ventilation.

3 Carefully pop out the bearings from your spinner. Keep them safe, away from paint and dust.

4 Decide what look you want to go for. Use the straw or wooden stirrer to flick paint for a messy look, or spray your spinner half and half (wait for the paint to dry before you spray the second half).

5 When the spinner is completely dry, push the bearings back in place. Your customized spinner is ready for action!

BEARINGS SPINNER

This DIY spinner is made using bearings and looks awesome. Try making one of your own!

YOU WILL NEED:

- 3 bearings (one slightly smaller than the others)
- A craft knife
- 5 plastic cable ties (or rubber bands)
- Scissors

HOW TO MAKE:

1 Have an adult use a craft knife to carefully remove the protector from the smallest bearing.

2 Put the three bearings in a row, placing the smaller one (without the protector) in the middle.

3 Next take three cable ties and tie them in a triangle shape around the bearings.

4 Tighten the cable ties until the bearings are completely tight. You can test whether it's solid by lifting the bearings by the cable ties.

5 Take two more cable ties and tighten them widthwise between the bearings. With the ties tightly in place, snip off the ends with some scissors.

6 Your spinner is ready for its speed test. Pick up the spinner with your thumb and index finger on either side of the middle bearing and give it a flick!

COIN UPGRADE

Modify your spinner using a couple of coins –
this simple upgrade will see it spin smoother
and make it easier to catch.

YOU WILL NEED:

- Electrical tape
- 2 10p coins
- A spinner with caps
- Scissors

HOW TO MAKE:

1 Cut a small piece of tape, then stick the ends together
to form a loop. The sticky side of the tape should be
on the outside.

2 Stick the tape to onto one of the spinner's caps.

3 Take one of the coins and stick it onto the tape. Use your thumb to hold down the coin firmly for a minute or two.

4 Make another loop of tape, stick the second coin to the other cap and hold it in place again.

5 Your turbo-charged spinner is ready to go— try a table spin to see the difference!

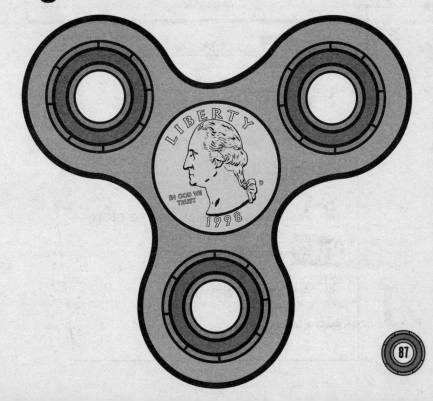

BOTTLE-TOP SPINNER

Don't waste your cash on a pricey spinner—create your own using bottle tops!

YOU WILL NEED:

 6 plastic bottle tops

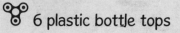 A glue gun or strong glue

A black marker

A straw or wooden coffee stirrer

A metal nail or skewer

A wooden skewer

Scissors

HOW TO MAKE:

1 Ask an adult to make a hole in the center of both caps, using a nail or skewer. Try using different-colored caps for a cool look.

2 Glue the two caps together by the flat sides, taking care not to get any glue in the holes.

3 Place three caps together around the outside of the spinner at equal distances. Mark a line on the center caps, as shown.

4 Glue the caps over the pen lines, in the middle of your construction. Then leave your spinner to dry.

5 Cut a piece of the wooden skewer the width of three bottle tops and push it through the holes. Add some glue around the holes to hold the stick in place.

6 Leave to dry again, then put your bottle-top spinner to the test.

DESIGN YOUR OWN SPINNER

Think you could do better than some of the designs out there? Plan out the different elements of your spinner, then draw a design for the ultimate fidget!

MATERIAL

- [ ] PLASTIC
- [ ] METAL
- [ ] WOOD

OTHER:

....

COLOR

....

NUMBER OF ARMS

....

CAPS

- [ ] YES - [ ] NO

SPECIAL FEATURES

....

....

WHAT'S NEXT?

Feeling spun out by spinners? Then why not try another way to fidget? Fidget sticks or a fidget cube offer brand-new ways to fidget.

FIDGET CUBE

Introducing the fidget cube! This gadget is perfect for fidgets who enjoy clicking, gliding, spinning and more. Fidget cubes have six sides with a different fidget feature on each one— which will be your favorite? These fun, easy-to-use little cubes are great for helping you to chill out.

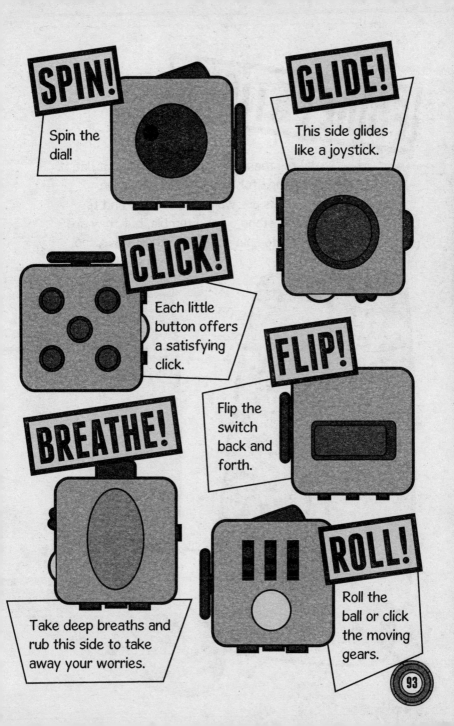

SPIN!
Spin the dial!

GLIDE!
This side glides like a joystick.

CLICK!
Each little button offers a satisfying click.

FLIP!
Flip the switch back and forth.

BREATHE!
Take deep breaths and rub this side to take away your worries.

ROLL!
Roll the ball or click the moving gears.

FIDGET STICKS

Gently roll these sticks end to end on a flat, hard surface for hours of fidgeting fun. Fidget sticks are weighted at each end to help them stand up and tumble, but they are satisfying to spin and roll on their sides, too.

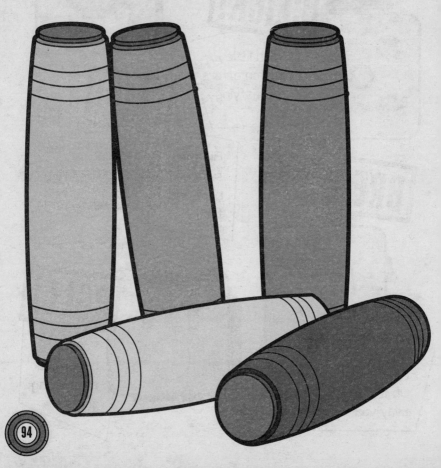

THREE TRICKS TO TRY

You can spin and roll fidget sticks whichever way you like. Try these tricks to get you started, or make up some of your own.

Flick the stick with your finger to make it roll back and forth, then catch it on the back of your hand.

BACKFLIP

HANDS FREE

Use another stick to push and hold your fidget stick.

DOUBLE TROUBLE

Take a stick in each hand and make them flip and roll in opposite directions.